Macmillan/McGraw-Hill TIMELINKS

All Together

PROGRAM AUTHORS
James A. Banks
Kevin P. Colleary
Linda Greenow
Walter C. Parker
Emily M. Schell
Dinah Zike

CONTRIBUTORS
Raymond C. Jones
Irma M. Olmedo

 Macmillan/McGraw-Hill

History

PROGRAM AUTHORS

James A. Banks, Ph.D.
Kerry and Linda Killinger Professor
  of Diversity Studies and Director, Center
  for Multicultural Education
University of Washington
Seattle, Washington

Kevin P. Colleary, Ed.D.
Curriculum and Teaching Department
Graduate School of Education
Fordham University
New York, New York

Linda Greenow, Ph.D.
Associate Professor and Chair
Department of Geography
State University of New York at New Paltz
New Paltz, New York

Walter C. Parker, Ph.D.
Professor of Social Studies Education,
  Adjunct Professor of Political Science
University of Washington
Seattle, Washington

Emily M. Schell, Ed.D.
Visiting Professor, Teacher Education
San Diego State University
San Diego, California

Dinah Zike
Educational Consultant
Dinah-Mite Activities, Inc.
San Antonio, Texas

CONTRIBUTORS

Raymond C. Jones, Ph.D.
Director of Secondary Social Studies
  Education
Wake Forest University
Winston-Salem, North Carolina

Irma M. Olmedo
Associate Professor
University of Illinois-Chicago
College of Education
Chicago, Illinois

HISTORIANS/SCHOLARS

Ned Blackhawk
Associate Professor of History
  and American Indian Studies
University of Wisconsin
Madison, Wisconsin

Jeffery D. Long, Ph.D.
Associate Professor of Religious
  and Asian Studies
Elizabethtown College
Elizabethtown, Pennsylvania

Oscar J. Martinez, Ph.D.
Regents Professor of History
University of Arizona
Tucson, Arizona

GRADE LEVEL REVIEWERS

Robin Bastolla
First Grade Teacher
Warnsdorfer School
East Brunswick, New Jersey

Kathleen Rose
First Grade Teacher
Bellerive Elementary School
St. Louis, Missouri

EDITORIAL ADVISORY BOARD

Bradley R. Bakle
Assistant Superintendent
East Allen County Schools
New Haven, Indiana

Marilyn Barr
Assistant Superintendent for Instruction
Clyde-Savannah Central School
Clyde, New York

Lisa Bogle
Elementary Coordinator, K-5
Rutherford County Schools
Murfreesboro, Tennessee

Janice Buselt
Campus Support, Primary and ESOL
Wichita Public Schools
Wichita, Kansas

Kathy Cassioppi
Social Studies Coordinator
Rockford Public Schools, District 205
Rockford, Illinois

Denise Johnson, Ph.D.
Social Studies Supervisor
Knox County Schools
Knoxville, Tennessee

Steven Klein, Ph.D.
Social Studies Coordinator
Illinois School District U-46
Elgin, Illinois

Sondra Markman
Curriculum Director
Warren Township Board of Education
Warren Township, New Jersey

Cathy Nelson
Social Studies Coordinator
Columbus Public Schools
Columbus, Ohio

Holly Pies
Social Studies Coordinator
Vigo County Schools
Terre Haute, Indiana

Avon Ruffin
Social Studies County Supervisor
Winston-Salem/Forsyth Schools
Lewisville, North Carolina

Chuck Schierloh
Social Studies Curriculum Team Leader
Lima City Schools
Lima, Ohio

Bob Shamy
Social Studies Supervisor
East Brunswick Public Schools
East Brunswick, New Jersey

Judy Trujillo
Social Studies Coordinator
Columbia Missouri School District
Columbia, Missouri

Gayle Voyles
Director of the Center for Economic
  Education
Kansas City School District
Kansas City, Missouri

Todd Wigginton
Coordinator of Social Studies K-12
Metropolitan Nashville Public Schools
Nashville, Tennessee

Students with print disabilities may be eligible to obtain an accessible, audio version of the pupil edition of this textbook. Please call Recording for the Blind & Dyslexic at 1-800-221-4792 for complete information.

All Together

Table of Contents

Unit 3 Life Long Ago

How did people live long ago?

How did people live long ago?	1
People, Places, and Events	2
Lesson 1 Families Long Ago	4
Place A Farmhouse Long Ago	7
Chart and Graph Skills Time Line	8
Lesson 2 The First Americans	10
Citizenship Points of View How do you help your family?	16
Lesson 3 Coming to America	18
Event Columbus Takes Land	21
Lesson 4 The Pilgrims	24
Map and Globe Skills Use History Maps	28
Lesson 5 People Keep America Free	30
Around the World India	33
People Coretta Scott King	36
Review and Assess	38
Picture Glossary	R1
Index	R3
Credits/Acknowledgments	R4

Skills and Features

Map and Globe Skills
Use History Maps 28

Chart and Graph Skills
Time Line 8

People, Places, and Events
Place A Farmhouse Long Ago 7
Event Columbus Takes Land 21
People Coretta Scott King 36

Around the World India 33

Citizenship Points of View
How do you help your family? 16

Maps

Troy, Ohio, Locator Map 16
The Pilgrims Sail to America, 1620 28
Two Native American Groups, 1700 39

Unit 3

EXPLORE The Big Idea

How did people live long ago?

LOG ON

Find out more about people long ago at www.macmillanmh.com

Life Long Ago

People, Places, and Events

The Pilgrims

The **Pilgrims** sailed from England to live in America.

For more about People, Places, and Events, visit
www.macmillanmh.com

Plymouth

Plymouth is the place where the Pilgrims lived.

The Pilgrims' First Thanksgiving

The Pilgrims had a feast called **Thanksgiving**.

3

Lesson 1

Vocabulary

interview

time line

Reading Skill

Compare and Contrast

Different   Alike   Different

Families Long Ago

A Family Interview

Jim's Grandma Bella lived on a farm long ago. Jim wondered what her life was like when she was a young girl.

Jim got an idea! He would **interview** Grandma Bella. To interview means to ask a person questions and to write down the answers.

 What is an interview?

My Interview with Bella

Jim What was life like on the farm when you were young?

Bella We didn't have a refrigerator. We had to put a block of ice into an ice box to keep our food cold. My little brother got in trouble for leaving the door open!

Jim What did your father do?

Bella My father was a farmer. He planted corn and wheat.

Jim Did you have chores?

Bella Oh, yes! Every day, before going to school, I fed the chickens.

 How is keeping food cold different today from long ago?

Places
A Farmhouse Long Ago

This is a farmhouse from long ago. There was only one water faucet in this farmhouse. It was located in the kitchen!

This is a time line of Bella's story. A **time line** shows the order of when things happen.

Age 4

Bella's Time Line

Jim What was school like?

Bella My whole school was only one room! Older kids helped little ones. We wrote with pens dipped in ink.

Jim What did you do at recess?

Bella We climbed trees. We played games like *Hide and Seek,* too!

| Age 6 | Age 9 |

 What did Bella do at recess?

Check Understanding

1. **Vocabulary** What is a **time line**?

2. **Compare and Contrast** How is school today and long ago alike? Different?

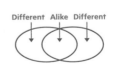

Different Alike Different

3. **EXPLORE The Big Idea** What was a farm like long ago?

The First Americans

Lesson 2

Vocabulary
Native
American

Reading Skill
Compare and
Contrast

Different Alike Different

Long Ago

Native Americans lived long, long ago, right where you live now. They were the first people to live in North America. They are also called American Indians.

 Who were the first people to live in North America?

long ago

today

Two Native American Groups

There were many Native American groups. Two of these groups were the Cherokee and the Chippewa. They lived near lakes and rivers.

The Cherokee made homes out of wood, mud, and grass. Chippewa homes were made from tree bark.

Cherokee home

Chippewa home

lake

fish

canoe

net

Chippewa girls and boys helped their families. The girls gathered nuts and rice. They also made clothes from animal skins. The boys helped hunt and fish.

 How did Chippewa boys help their families?

A Cherokee Family Today

Meet Wilma. Wilma is a Cherokee girl who lives in Ohio. Long ago, Wilma's family lived in Tennessee.

Wilma's mom tells stories about their family from Tennessee. The boys hunted with bows and arrows. The girls made clay bowls and helped their mothers sew.

Today, Wilma helps her family just like girls did in Tennessee long ago. She helps her grandpa cut the lawn.

 How is Wilma like the Cherokee girls of long ago?

Check Understanding

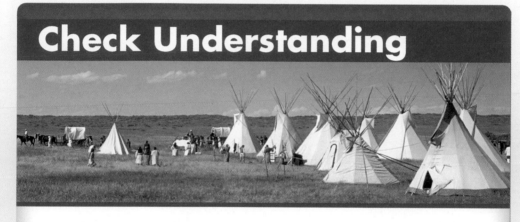

1. **Vocabulary** What are the names of some **Native American** groups?

2. **Compare and Contrast** How were the Cherokee and Chippewa homes alike? Different?

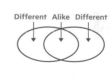
Different Alike Different

3. How did Native American children live long ago?

Citizenship

Points of View

How do you help your family?

These first graders are from Concord Elementary School in Troy, Ohio. Read about how they help and care for their families.

Troy, Ohio

"When my mother looks tired, I help her fold the laundry. I hold the door for my grandpa when he walks with his cane."

Niki Krishnan

Niki Krishnan

"Sometimes I help with dinner by cutting up the cheese for my macaroni. I also take out the trash and help Granny in the garden."

Isiah Sandridge
Isiah Sandridge

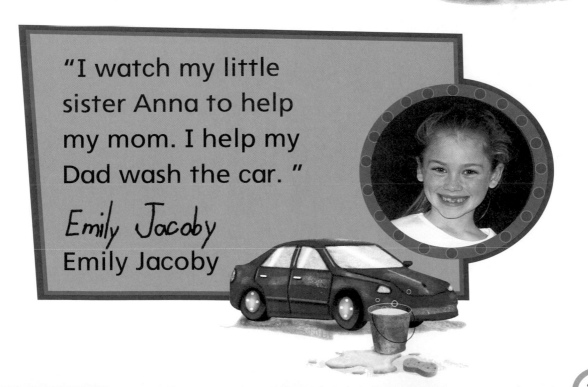

"I watch my little sister Anna to help my mom. I help my Dad wash the car."

Emily Jacoby
Emily Jacoby

Coming to America

Lesson 3

Vocabulary

settler

Reading Skill

Compare and Contrast

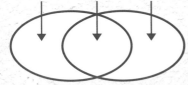

Different Alike Different

Three Ships Sail

Long ago, a Native American group called the Taino lived on an island near North America. The Taino were farmers and fishers. They planted corn. They fished for food.

One day the Taino looked out on the Atlantic Ocean. Three ships with white sails were close by.

How did the Taino get food?

Columbus Arrives

The ships were called the *Nina,* the *Pinta,* and the *Santa Maria.* Christopher Columbus was the captain of the ships. He and his men were searching for gold.

Columbus and his men were almost out of food and water when they saw land. The Taino paddled out to help them.

Later, Columbus gave the Taino glass beads and brass bells. The Taino gave Columbus and his men gifts of parrots and gold.

 What did Columbus give to the Taino?

Event
Columbus Takes Land

Columbus put the Spanish flag on the Taino land. He said that the land now belonged to Spain.

Settlers Arrive

After Columbus, other people sailed across the Atlantic Ocean to America. Some decided to make America their home. They were called **settlers**.

The first settlers to move to America were from Spain. They moved to an area in Florida. They called this place St. Augustine. Today, St. Augustine is the oldest city in the United States.

 Where is St. Augustine?

Check Understanding

1. **Vocabulary** What country did the first **settlers** come from?

2. **Compare and Contrast** How were Columbus and the settlers alike? Different?

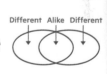
Different   Alike   Different

3. What happened to the Taino land?

Lesson 4

Vocabulary
Pilgrim

Reading Skill
Compare and Contrast

Different   Alike   Different

The Pilgrims

The Pilgrims Come

Another group of settlers was called the **Pilgrims**. They came from England to America for a better life. The Pilgrims built a town called Plymouth.

 Why did the Pilgrims come to America?

Native Americans Help

The Pilgrims had a hard winter.
They did not know how to hunt and
grow food in this new land. Some
Native Americans helped them.
Soon the Pilgrims had food to eat.

The Pilgrims wanted to thank God for all that had happened. They invited the Native Americans to a great feast. This was the Pilgrims' first Thanksgiving.

 Why did the Pilgrims have a feast?

Check Understanding

1. **Vocabulary** Who were the **Pilgrims**?

2. **Compare and Contrast** How were the Native Americans and Pilgrims alike? Different?

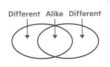
Different Alike Different

3. **EXPLORE The Big Idea** How did the Native Americans help the Pilgrims?

Map and Globe Skills

Use History Maps

Vocabulary
history map

A **history map** shows places or paths from long ago. Look at the history map below. It shows the path that the Pilgrims took.

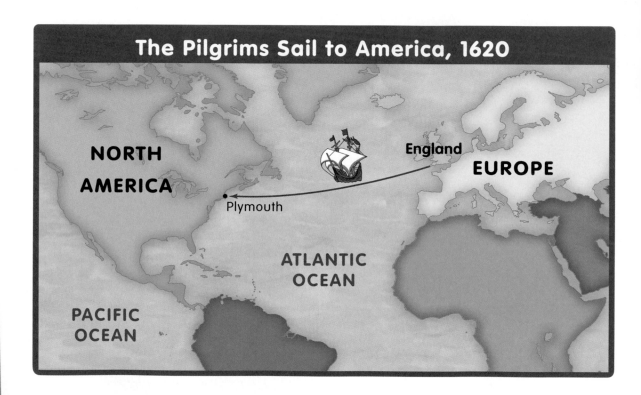

The Pilgrims Sail to America, 1620

NORTH AMERICA

England

EUROPE

Plymouth

ATLANTIC OCEAN

PACIFIC OCEAN

The Pilgrims sailed from England to Plymouth on a ship called the *Mayflower*.

Try the Skill

1. What does a **history map** show?

2. From what continent did the Pilgrims come?

Writing Activity Suppose you took a trip across the ocean. Write a story about your trip.

People Keep America Free

Vocabulary

President

slavery

immigrant

Reading Skill

Compare and Contrast

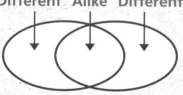

Different   Alike   Different

A Free Country

More settlers came from England to live in America. Most wanted to be free from England.

The settlers had a war with England. George Washington helped America win the war. Later, he became America's first **President**. The President is the leader of our country.

 Who was George Washington?

Freedom for Everyone

Years later, another great President cared about freedom. His name was Abraham Lincoln. He knew that **slavery** was wrong. Slavery is one person taking away another person's freedom.

Some people in our country wanted to end slavery. Others did not. People in some states fought against people in other states. It was called the Civil War. When the war ended, slavery ended.

What is slavery?

Around the World

Freedom is important all around the world. This girl from India celebrates her country's freedom.

Freedom Across America

After the Civil War, some areas became crowded with people. Families moved further west for more room. The United States grew larger and larger.

People continued to come from other countries for freedom and a better life. They were called **immigrants**.

Some immigrants arrived on ships to Ellis Island in New York. They could see the Statue of Liberty.

The Statue of Liberty stands for freedom. It was a gift to the United States from France.

Who are immigrants?

Marching for Freedom

Not long ago, black children could not go to school with white children. Dr. Martin Luther King, Jr., gave speeches and went on marches to change this.

People
Coretta Scott King

Coretta was the wife of Martin Luther King, Jr. She said, "We . . . dream of a world being reborn in freedom."

Today all children go to school together. In America, we must work toward freedom today, just as we did long ago.

 What did Martin Luther King, Jr., want to change?

Check Understanding

1. **Vocabulary** What does our **President** do?

2. **Compare and Contrast** How were George Washington and Abraham Lincoln alike? Different?

   Different Alike Different

3. 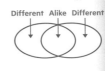 How did Martin Luther King, Jr., help children?

Unit 3 Review and Assess

Vocabulary

Complete each sentence.

interview   slavery   immigrant

1. A person who comes from another country to live here is called an _____.

2. An _____ is asking questions and writing down the answers.

3. _____ is one person taking away another person's freedom.

Critical Thinking

4. How can interviewing an older person help us find out about long ago?

5. Why is freedom important?

Skill

Use History Maps

Look at the map of Georgia.
Answer the question below.

Two Native American Groups, 1700

Cherokee

Shawnee

Georgia

ATLANTIC OCEAN

6. What two Native American groups lived in Georgia in 1700?

   A. The Shawnee and the Cherokee

   B. The Shawnee and the Taino

   C. The Shawnee and the Hopi

History Activity

Make a Mobile

1 Draw pictures of people, places, and events from long ago.

2 Turn each picture over. Write a sentence telling what you learned.

3 Attach your pictures to a coat hanger.

4 Share your mobile with your class.

The Statue of Liberty is on Liberty Island.

Picture Glossary

H

history map A **history map** shows places or paths from long ago. (page 28)

I

immigrant An **immigrant** is a person who comes from another country for freedom and a better life. (page 34)

interview To **interview** means to ask a person questions and to write down the answers. (page 5)

N

Native American **Native Americans** were the first people to live in North America. (page 11)

P

Pilgrim **Pilgrims** were settlers from England who came to America for a better life. (page 25)

President The **President** is the leader of our country. (page 31)

settler A **settler** is a person who came to live in America long ago. (page 22)

slavery **Slavery** is one person taking away another person's freedom. (page 32)

time line A **time line** is a line that shows the order of when things happen. (page 8)

Age 9

Age 6

Age 4

Index

This index lists many things you can find in your book. It tells the page numbers on which they are found. If you see the letter *m* before a page number, you will find a map on that page.

A

African Americans, 36–37
America, 18–23, 30–37
  See also United
    States of America
  and Columbus, 19–21
  freedom in, 31–33,
    34–35, 36–37
  and immigrants, 34–35
  and Native Americans,
    10–15, 39
  and Pilgrims, 2–3,
    24–27, 28–29
  and settlers, 22–23, 31
  and slavery, 32–33
  trip to, *m28*, 28–29
American Indians,
  10–15, 39. *See also*
    Native Americans
Animals, 7, 13
Around the World, 33
Atlantic Ocean
  and Columbus, 19
  map, *m28*
  and settlers, 22

C

Canoes, 13
Cherokee, 12, 14–15
Chippewa, 12–13
Chores, 7
Citizenship
  Points of View, 16–17
Civil War, 33–34
Clothes, 13
Columbus, Christopher,
  19–22
Concord Elementary
  School, Troy, Ohio,
  16–17

E

Ellis Island, New York, 35
England
  and Pilgrims, 2, 25,
    m28, 29
  war with, 31
Europe, *m28*

F

Families, 4–9
  helping, 13, 14–15, 16–17
  interviews, 5–8
  of Native Americans,
    13, 14–15
Farms, life on, 5–8
First Americans, 10–11.
  See also Native
    Americans
Fish, 13
Florida, 23
Food
  of farming families, 6
  of Native Americans,
    13, 19
  of Pilgrims, 26–27
France, 35
Freedom in America
  and immigrants, 34–35
  and settlers, 31
  and slavery, 32–33
  and Statue of Liberty, 35
  war for, 31, 33
  working for, 36–37

G

Georgia, 39
Gold, 20–21

H

Helping our families
  in Native American
    families, 13, 14–15
  ways we help, 15, 16–17
History maps, *m28*
Homes
  of farming families, 7
  of Native Americans, 12

I

Ice boxes, 6
Immigrants, 34–35
India, 33
Interviews, 5–8

K

King, Coretta Scott, 36
King, Martin Luther, Jr.,
  36–37

L

Lakes, 13
Lincoln, Abraham, 32

M

Map and Globe Skills,
  m28, 28–29, *m39*
Mayflower, 29
Mobiles, making, 40

N

Native Americans, 10–15,
  39
  about, 11
  Cherokee, 12, 14–15
  Chippewa, 12–13
  and Columbus, 19, 21
  family life of, 13, 14–15
  food of, 13, 19
  and Pilgrims, 26–27
Taino, 19
Nets, 13
New York, 35
Nina, 20
North America, 19, *m28*

O

Ohio, 14

Index

P

People, Places, and Events, 2–3
Pilgrims, 24–27
  about, 25
  food of, 26–27
  and Native Americans, 26–27
  and Plymouth, 3, 25, *m28*
  and Thanksgiving, 3, 27
  trip of, 2, *m28,* 29
Pinta, 20
Plymouth, 3, 25, *m28*
Points of View, 16–17

Presidents of the United States, 31, 32

R

Refrigerators, 6

S

Santa Maria, 20
School, 8, 36–37
Settlers in America, 22–23, 31
Slavery, 32–33
Spain, 21, 23
Statue of Liberty, 35

St. Augustine, Florida, 23

T

Taino, 19, 21
Tennessee, 14
Thanksgiving, 3, 27
Time lines, 8–9

U

United States of America. *See also* America
  and immigrants, 34–35
  moving west, 34
  oldest city, 23

Presidents of the United States, 31–32
  and slavery, 32–33
  and Statue of Liberty, 35
  wars for freedom, 31, 33

W

Washington, George, 31
West, moving to the, 34

Credits

Maps: XNR

Illustrations: 8-9: Ellen Beier. 24-25: Johanna Van Der Sterre. 6-7: Krstin Varner.

Photography Credits: All Photographs are by Macmillan/McGraw-hill (MMH) except as noted below.

1: Gabe Palmer/Alamy Images. 2: (br) Marilyn Angel Wynn/Nativestock Pictures; (l) Farrell Grehan/CORBIS; (tr) Marilyn Angel Wynn/Nativestock Pictures. 3: (bl) Bettmann/CORBIS; (br) Burke/Getty Images; (t) Swerve/Alamy Images. 4: Bettmann/CORBIS. 5: (bl) Jens Honore Photography Ltd/Getty Images; (br) image100/PunchStock; (t) C Squared Studios/Getty Images. 6: (bc) CORBIS; (br) Underwood & Underwood/CORBIS. 7: (b) William A. Bake/CORBIS; (t) G.K. & Vikki Hart/Getty Images. 9: (c) Bettmann/CORBIS. 10: Lindsay Hebberd/CORBIS. 11: (l) Brian A. Vikander/CORBIS; (r) Dana Hoff/Beateworks/CORBIS. 14: Lawrence Migdale Photography. 15: Brian A. Vikander/CORBIS. 16: (l) Gail Bulach/Concord Elementary School. 17: (br) Gail Bulach/Concord Elementary School; (tl) Gail Bulach/Concord Elementary School. 18: Digishooter/Fotolia. 19: (bl) Index Stock Imagery. 21: (t) Martin Harvey/Alamy Images. 26: Bettmann/CORBIS. 29: Bettmann/CORBIS. 30: Philadelphia Museum of Art/CORBIS. 31: The Granger Collection, New York. 32: Francis G. Mayer/CORBIS. 33: (b) Richard Levine/Alamy Images. 33: (bkgd) DESAI NOSHIR/CORBIS. 33: (t) From the original painting by Mort Künstler copyright 2002. 34: American Stock/Hulton Archive/Getty Images. 35: (bkgd) Jose Fuste Raga/hCORBIS; (l) Bettmann/CORBIS; (r) John Wang/Getty Images. 36: (b) Erik S. Lesser/Getty Images; (t) Ivan Massar/Stock Photo. 37: The Granger Collection, New York. 38: C Squared Studios/Getty Images. 40: (t) Stockdisc/PunchStock. R1: (c) Jens Honore Photography Ltd/Getty Images; (cr) C Squared Studios/Getty Images; (tc) Bettmann/CORBIS. R2: (t) Sygma/CORBIS.